BEST OF BRITAIN

Contents

History of Britain	6
Early Britain	12
Castles	14
Cathedrals and Abbeys	18
Medieval Towns and Colleges	24
Moors, Mountains and Countryside	28
Royal Residences	33
Stately Homes and Gardens	36
Rivers, Canals and Lakes	42
Historic Towns and Cities	46
Traditions and Ceremonies	50
Coasts and Seaside	56
Modern Britain	60
Index	64

Publication in this form © Jarrold Publishing Ltd 2001, latest reprint 2002.

All rights reserved. No part of this publication may be reproduced, stored in a retrieval system, or transmitted, in any form or by any means, electronic, mechanical, photocopying, recording or otherwise, without prior permission of Jarrold Publishing and the copyright holders.

Written by Peter Brimacombe. The author has asserted his moral rights.
Edited by Angela Royston.
Designed by Simon Borrough.
Front cover designed by John Buckley.

Printed in Singapore.
ISBN 1 871004 88 8 (hardback)
ISBN 1 871004 87 X (paperback)   2/02

Acknowledgements:
Photographs courtesy of www.britainonview.com, the photography library of the British Tourist Authority, Peter Brimacombe and Jarrold Publishing, with additional photography by Mike Caldwell, Canterbury Cathedral Enterprises Ltd, Colorsport, John Crook, Mary Evans, Tim Graham Picture Library, John Heseltine, Keith Hunter, Imperial War Museum, Sam Lloyd, Robert Royston and Science & Society Picture Library.

Front cover:
Stonehenge, one of Britain's best-known landmarks, occupies an isolated site in the middle of Salisbury Plain in southern England. It is designated a World Heritage Site.

Previous pages:
Few places in Britain exude a greater air of mystery and romance than the Isle of Skye, off the north-west coast of Scotland, evoking images of Bonnie Prince Charlie and Flora MacDonald. The mountains beyond the loch are the Cuillins with peaks more than 900 metres (3,000 feet) high.

Opposite:
Nelson's Column in Trafalgar Square stands at the heart of London's West End. It was built to commemorate Nelson's naval victory at the Battle of Trafalgar in 1805.

Back cover:
Royal Crescent in Bath, designed by John Wood the Younger in 1767.

History of Britain

Britain is an island kingdom which has evolved over thousands of years, swept along on a tide of decisive events, steered by inspirational leaders who came from all corners of the nation, and some from overseas. Over the centuries a handful of men and women have guided the fortunes of a relatively small nation, one that continues to earn respect throughout the world in the 21st century.

Medieval Britain

Britain as it is today essentially began in 1066 after William the Conqueror crossed over from Normandy and, using a combination of superior tactics and weaponry, annihilated the English King Harold's army near the small south-coast town of Hastings. Three months later William, the bastard son of Robert the Devil and a tanner's daughter from Falaise, was crowned in Westminster Abbey. He then proceeded to take Anglo-Saxon England out of the Dark Ages, ruthlessly converting a loosely knit group of primitive regional kingdoms into a sophisticated unified nation with efficient central administration, law and order and, above all, a pride and purpose to ensure that it was never conquered again.

William instigated Medieval England, an exuberant, eclectic kingdom in which soldiers, scholars and churchmen doubled as statesmen. Their legacy is the Domesday Book, Magna Carta and the magnificent range of castles and cathedrals which continue to

William the Conqueror founded Battle Abbey on the site of his famous victory over King Harold's Anglo-Saxon army near Hastings in 1066. The site is well preserved and maintained by English Heritage.

Edward I built Caernarfon Castle to subdue the Welsh in the late 13th century. In 1969 it was the setting for the investiture of HRH Prince Charles as the 21st Prince of Wales, a title created by King Edward whose son was born at the castle and became the first Prince of Wales.

dominate the landscape many centuries later. Some of Britain's most enduring landmarks – the Tower of London, Durham Cathedral and St Michael's Mount – date from William's time on the English throne.

William's successors wished to control more than merely England: monarchs such as Henry II and Edward I extended their activities into Scotland and Wales. Henry ruled over England's first overseas empire which spread from the Arctic to the Pyrenees and included significant parts of France and Ireland. However, the Welsh and Scots were reluctant to join, even keener to leave. Fervent patriots such as Llewellyn and Robert the Bruce managed to expel the English, but not for long.

The Middle Ages are generally considered to have ended with the Battle of Bosworth in 1485 when the Welshman Henry Tudor defeated the English King Richard III, thereby ending the Wars of the Roses, a long running civil conflict which ruined the nation and lost it its French territories.

The dramatic statue of the Scottish hero Robert the Bruce stands on the site of the Battle of Bannockburn near Stirling, where he decisively defeated the English army of Edward II in the summer of 1314, thereby regaining independence for Scotland.

THE TUDORS

Henry Tudor was crowned King Henry VII and brought much needed stability to England and Wales, although his son Henry VIII fomented religious dissension: to obtain a divorce from his first wife, he broke away from the Pope in Rome and declared himself head of the church in England.

He was succeeded by Edward and Mary, who both proved to be disastrous rulers and left no heirs. Thus in 1558 Henry VIII's younger daughter, Elizabeth, inherited a weak, dispirited and divided country, yet developed into an outstanding leader with a natural ability to choose and motivate capable men to the benefit of her kingdom. Assisted by Lord Burghley, Francis Drake and others, Elizabeth slowly but surely made England a major power – combative and assertive, capable of resisting invasion from Spain, at that time the world's most powerful nation. The Tudors completed the conquest of Ireland but not without significant bloodshed.

King Henry VIII is best known for his massive size and many wives. His second daughter, Elizabeth, survived perilous times to become one of the nation's greatest ever monarchs.

The scene of many of Shakespeare's plays, the original Globe on the south bank of the Thames was accidentally burnt to the ground in 1613, during a production of Henry VIII. *Recently a replica of Shakespeare's Globe has been built near the site of the original.*

Elizabeth's lasting legacy was the permanent foundation of the Anglican Church. She also established England as a literary nation by encouraging dramatists such as William Shakespeare, the greatest playwright the world has ever seen. The Elizabethan era was a time of great personal self-esteem and prosperity, which resulted in the first of the nation's great stately homes – Burghley, Hardwick and Longleat. Tudor England was also an age of great scholarship, witnessing the foundation of colleges such as Christ Church at Oxford, and Trinity and Emmanuel at Cambridge.

Drake's voyage around the world and the subsequent defeat of the Armada in 1588 launched the nation's reputation as a major maritime power, whilst the foundation of the East India Company initiated the British Empire.

History of Britain

King versus Parliament

Elizabeth's major failure was her inability to produce an heir, thus in 1603 Scotland's King James VI became the first ruler of Great Britain. The resultant disastrous reigns of four successive Stuart kings brought equal, if not greater, misery to Scotland than England. Charles I's inability to appreciate the importance of parliament and democracy plunged the nation into a bitter civil war, which ended with the monarch's public execution in 1649. Britain became a republic for the only time in its history.

A hitherto obscure, middle-aged country squire named Oliver Cromwell had become leader of the Parliamentary army. Cromwell possessed no combat or leadership experience yet displayed a clarity of vision and decisiveness of action that is the hallmark of a great military commander. He transformed traditional, almost feudal, troop formations into the New Model Army, the first professional army and a highly disciplined and motivated fighting machine. It decisively defeated the Royalist forces under King Charles. Less creditable, Cromwell's ruthless persecution of Irish Catholics has left a lasting and bitter legacy.

Cromwell reluctantly accepted the title Lord Protector, head of the embryonic republic, and ensured that Britain would always remain a democracy by maintaining parliament with a freely elected House of Commons. After the monarchy was restored in 1660 it became constitutional unlike the previous autocratic institution. This pioneering concept gave the nation a considerable head start over the rest of Europe and contributed to Britain's later influential position in the world.

In 1688 King James II was deposed and William of Orange invited over from Holland to become king. Orangemen in Ireland still celebrate William's victory over James at the Battle of the Boyne two years later.

Eighteenth-century Glory

When William died, his sister-in-law Anne inherited the throne. During her reign John Churchill, the 1st Duke of Marlborough, won the Battle of Blenheim and a series of other continental victories, completely crushing the armies of the French King Louis XIV, the Sun King. The formal process of establishing the United Kingdom continued in 1707 with the Act of Union between England and Scotland. The unification of the Scottish and English parliaments was followed in 1801 by a similar Act of Union between

A statue of Oliver Cromwell stands outside the Houses of Parliament, whose rights he strove so hard to maintain during the mid 17th century. In the background is Big Ben, one of London's most famous landmarks.

England and Ireland. Bonnie Prince Charlie's abortive Jacobite uprising ended with his defeat at Culloden in 1746 and in misery and humiliation for Scotland during the Highland Clearances.

But the 18th century was largely peaceful at home and many great stately homes were built, including Marlborough's own Blenheim Palace, Houghton Hall, Castle Howard and Hopetoun House in Scotland. During this architectural golden age, St Paul's Cathedral, Wren's greatest masterpiece, was also completed.

At the end of the century Britain was again threatened with invasion, this time by Napoleon. Nelson and Wellington, two outstanding military commanders, opposed him. Nelson was a naval genius: a combination of meticulous planning, vastly superior gunnery, brilliantly unorthodox tactics and raw courage enabled Britain's greatest admiral to achieve a series of dazzling victories at sea, culminating in 1805 with the Battle of Trafalgar. Nelson never lost a battle, not even a ship, and Britain was saved from invasion. Ten years later the Irish-born general, Wellington, whose army contained several Highland regiments, finally defeated Napoleon at Waterloo.

HMS Victory, *Nelson's flagship at the Battle of Trafalgar in 1805, is now berthed in Portsmouth Dockyard, providing a fitting memorial to the nation's greatest admiral, who was fatally shot whilst fighting that epic battle against the French fleet.*

Industry and Empire

There followed 100 years of unparalleled peace and prosperity with Britain at its peak of power and prestige. This was the time of the Industrial Revolution and the introduction of the railways. By the end of the 19th century Queen Victoria ruled more than a quarter of the globe. Yet Britain's role of leading world power was already being challenged by America and in Europe. The First World War wreaked destruction not only on people's lives but on Europe and Britain's economy. Lloyd George, a charismatic Welshman, led Britain through this very difficult time. It was not long, however, before Britain was facing its greatest ever threat – Adolf Hitler.

The invention of the steam train was one of the great technological feats of the 19th century. Mallard, *the fastest steam locomotive of all time, is now on display in the National Railway Museum in York.*

History of Britain

Second World War

In 1940 the United Kingdom was singularly ill prepared to meet the mighty German armies which had already conquered much of Europe. France had fallen and Britain stood alone, with its defences woefully weak. At this hour of maximum danger, Winston Churchill gave the country courage and the will to resist: 'We shall defend our island, whatever the cost may be. We shall fight on the beaches, we shall fight on the landing grounds, we shall fight in the fields and in the streets, we shall fight in the hills, we shall never surrender.' Aided by a small number of incredibly brave fighter pilots, the threat of invasion was held at bay and Hitler turned his attention to invading Russia instead. Skillfully exploiting his friendship with President Roosevelt, Churchill succeeded in persuading America to enter the war. Gradually the tide turned and a devastated Germany ultimately capitulated in 1945.

Spitfires and Hurricanes, the fighter planes that prevented Hitler invading Britain in the summer of 1940, can be seen together with other Second World War combat aircraft in a special exhibition in the Imperial War Museum at Duxford in Cambridgeshire.

Modern Britain

Today, in a nuclear age, the menace of the Cold War has come and gone and Europe has been largely at peace for over 50 years. In common with other European nations Britain no longer has an overseas empire and is in the middle of profound social, political and technological change. Welsh and Scottish desires for devolution are redefining the political make-up of the United Kingdom, southern Ireland having become an independent state in 1921. As the European Union becomes larger and more powerful, Britain must decide whether to join economically and politically with its European neighbours or remain independent on the sidelines. Whatever the challenges, Britain will rely on its democratic institutions and inspirational individuals to provide fair and successful solutions.

The Lloyds of London building in the City of London, constructed in 1986 by the internationally renowned British architect Richard Rogers, symbolises the spirit of the new architecture to be found in Britain – confident, assertive, high-tech and highly functional.

Early Britain

Enigmatic prehistoric monuments, such as Callinish and the Ring of Brodgar in the Scottish Isles, Castlerigg in the Lake District, Avebury and Stonehenge in southern England, indicate that civilisation existed in Britain thousands of years ago. Incredible feats of engineering at the time, their precise function remains a mystery. But huge burial mounds on Dartmoor and Salisbury Plain, such as West Kennet Long Barrow, seem to indicate the desire of neolithic people to honour their dead.

There are many reminders of the Romans' occupation of Britain ranging from Hadrian's Wall, built to keep out the Scots, to the Roman baths in Bath, created for more pleasurable pursuits. Celtic crosses in northern and western Britain show that the flickering flame of Christianity was kept alive during the Dark Ages after the Romans withdrew from the British Isles in AD 407.

The construction of Stonehenge on Salisbury Plain is thought to have commenced some 5,000 years ago and been finished around 1600 BC. When the Romans arrived in AD 43 they found it had been abandoned. 'Stonehenge' derives from the Saxon word Stanhengist, 'the place of the hanging stones'.

The neolithic burial chamber of Pentre Ifan is near the Preseli mountains in south-west Wales. In the late 17th century Pentre Ifan became known as Coetan Arthur – Arthur's Quoit. Fairies are said to dance here.

Callinish, on the Isle of Lewis off the coast of northern Scotland, stands on a lonely promontory on the shores of East Loch Roag. Although the stones are visible from far away, their many shades of grey and pink can only be seen close to. They were probably raised some 4,000 years ago.

This Celtic cross is located on Iona, an island off the west coast of Scotland. St Columba travelled here from Ireland to establish a monastery in 563, and take Christianity into the rest of Scotland. The faith later spread south to Northumbria and Lindisfarne.

Hadrian's Wall (below) is named after the emperor who built it, to mark the northern frontier of the Roman occupation. Constructed over a five-year period beginning in AD 122, the wall stretches some 110 kilometres (70 miles) between the Solway and the Tyne, with stone ramparts up to 3 metres (10 feet) thick.

The Romans exploited the natural hot springs at Bath to build steaming hot baths, including the Great Bath, King's Bath and Queen's Bath. Today they represent some of the most important Roman remains in Britain.

Castles

Most castles to be found across Britain were built during the troubled times of the Middle Ages. William the Conqueror and his knights constructed the Tower of London and Chepstow Castle shortly after his arrival in 1066, the latter to guard his western frontier and keep out the marauding Welsh. These were the first secular stone buildings to be constructed by the Normans in their new kingdom.

Castles continued to be built over the next several centuries, invariably representing the latest in military technology. They were created either for protection, particularly on the borders between England and Scotland and England and Wales and on the Channel coast, or to impress and intimidate the local population in newly conquered territories. Castles remained an important military feature in Britain until finally made redundant in the 17th century, when many fortresses were laid waste by Oliver Cromwell's artillery.

Dover Castle is a medieval keep constructed in the reign of Henry II, and has a Roman lighthouse and a fine view of the famous white cliffs. Below ground in a complex maze of tunnels is a Second World War command and communication centre.

The Tower of London, begun by William the Conqueror, was originally a fortress and a royal palace, but it acquired a gruesome reputation as a prison and place of execution. Those entering through Traitor's Gate rarely returned. The Jacobite rebel, Lord Lovat, was the last person to be publicly beheaded at the Tower, in 1747.

Edward I built Conwy Castle (below) in 1288 after he had conquered Wales. It is now a World Heritage Site and one of the most impressive castles in the whole of Britain. The castellated turrets of the 19th-century suspension bridge, constructed by Scottish engineer Thomas Telford, match those of the castle.

Caerphilly Castle in south Wales (above) has proved impregnable since it was rebuilt in 1271 by 'Red Gilbert' de Clare, Anglo-Norman Lord of Glamorgan. It is famous for its leaning tower and is by far the largest castle in Wales.

Dunvegan Castle on the northern tip of the Isle of Skye is the oldest home in Scotland to be continuously inhabited by one family, the Chiefs of the Clan MacLeod. Its curtain wall dates from the 12th century and John MacLeod of MacLeod is the 29th Chief of Clan.

CASTLES

Bodiam Castle in East Sussex faces south across the Sussex Marshes. It was built for Richard II at the end of the 14th century during the Hundred Years War, to protect the area from cross-channel raids by the French. Now this beautiful ruin is owned by The National Trust.

CASTLES

Clifford's Tower was once the keep of York Castle and stands on a large mound originally constructed by William the Conqueror as part of his defences for the city of York. There are panoramic views of the city from the top of the tower.

Harlech Castle was built by Edward I on the top of a towering rock overlooking Tremadog Bay on the west coast of Wales. The popular folk song 'Men of Harlech' dates from the siege of the castle by Yorkists during the Wars of the Roses.

Castle-building did not end with the Middle Ages – in the early 20th century Edwin Lutyens created Castle Drogo on Dartmoor for the self-made millionaire Julius Drewe.

Sudeley in Gloucestershire has a turbulent history. During the Wars of the Roses its owner was declared a traitor and his castle confiscated, while two successive Tudor owners were executed. During the Civil War it was besieged and left derelict for nearly 200 years. Today Sudeley enjoys a happier existence.

Warwick Castle in the Midlands is considered to be the finest medieval castle in England. Building commenced shortly after the Norman Conquest in 1068, when William the Conqueror created the first Earl of Warwick. It represents nearly 1,000 years of history.

Cathedrals and Abbeys

Medieval Britain was a far more religious country than today's Britain: the numerous cathedrals and abbeys – a testament to a fervent faith – remain architectural and engineering feats of the highest order. In an age of limited education, cathedrals were constructed as functional theatres in which to perform public acts of worship and impress the largely illiterate masses with dazzling displays of sound and colour.

The great period of cathedral construction in the new Gothic style took place between the 13th and mid 14th centuries. Ecclesiastical builders at that time were constantly exploring the upper limits of medieval technology. Sometimes they literally overreached themselves, particularly when creating that great architectural masterpiece, the spire: those at Lincoln and Malmesbury were too tall and came tumbling down. Nevertheless, cathedrals represent the best architectural achievement of Britain in the Middle Ages.

York Minster is the biggest medieval Gothic church in northern Europe and houses the largest collection of medieval glass in England. This clock was made in 1749 by Henry Hindley, a York clock-maker.

Canterbury Cathedral was founded in 597 and is the mother church of the nation's Anglican community. In 1170 it witnessed the martyrdom of Thomas Becket, murdered by Henry II's soldiers. The site of Becket's shrine is in the cathedral and this medieval stained-glass window (right) is thought to be of him.

The Cistercian abbey of Rievaulx was established at the head of a secluded valley in north Yorkshire during the 13th century. Today it is an evocative ruin.

The nation's monarchs have invariably been crowned at Westminster Abbey, from William the Conqueror in 1066 to HRH Queen Elizabeth II, whose coronation was held here in 1953. Many of the nation's great literary figures are buried at Poet's Corner within the Abbey.

Cathedrals and Abbeys

This Cistercian abbey at Tintern was founded in 1131. It was one of the many victims of Henry VIII's Dissolution of the Monasteries in 1536 and now lies in ruins on the Welsh bank of the River Wye between Chepstow and Monmouth.

The spire of Salisbury Cathedral – the tallest spire in Britain – looks like solid stone, but the stones are quite thin and overlay a wooden frame. Otherwise the load on the walls below would be too great.

Salisbury Cathedral's outstanding feature is its spire, standing more than 120 metres (400 feet) high. The cathedral is a magnificent example of Gothic architecture and its setting within the Cathedral Close, encircled by the River Avon, shows Britain at its best.

CATHEDRALS AND ABBEYS

St Davids in Pembroke, with its cathedral and impressive Bishop's Palace, is Britain's smallest city and is more than 800 years old. The sculpture (below) shows St David, the patron saint of Wales, who is commemorated on 1 March each year.

The cathedral at Chester (above) was originally a Benedictine monastery founded in 1092. It survived the Dissolution of the Monasteries and shortly afterwards became an Anglican cathedral. It displays an eclectic yet pleasing mixture of architecture.

The west front of the cathedral at Wells with its fine array of statuary presents a memorable sight across the Close in this small, attractive Somerset town. The Chapter House and the astronomical clock are notable features of this exquisite example of Gothic architecture.

CATHEDRALS AND ABBEYS

St Paul's Cathedral was built by Christopher Wren to replace the old Saxon cathedral which was destroyed during the Great Fire of London in 1666. Many state occasions have been held here, including the funerals of Lawrence of Arabia and Winston Churchill, and the wedding of HRH Prince Charles and Lady Diana Spencer.

The cathedral at Durham is one of the oldest in Britain and contains the remains of an eminent monk, the Venerable Bede. For many years the structure of the cathedral moved alarmingly, until the medieval mortar finally set.

In the 16th and 17th centuries people used the old cathedral of St Paul's as a short cut – they rode on horseback and drove their animals straight through it on their way to and from the River Thames.

Melrose Abbey, now a ruin, is where the heart of Robert the Bruce is buried. Melrose, on the Scottish Borders, was founded around 1136 as a Cistercian abbey. It was largely destroyed by King Richard II's English army in 1385.

Winchester, one of England's oldest cathedrals, was begun in 1079. St Swithun, Izaak Walton and Jane Austen are all buried here. The interior is rich in artistic treasures, including Anthony Gormley's recent, striking sculpture Sound II.

CATHEDRALS AND ABBEYS

The elaborate fan vaulting in the Cloister Walk is one of the many delightful features within the cathedral at Gloucester. Like many English cathedrals it was developed over a long period, taking nearly 300 years to complete from its foundation in the 11th century.

Medieval Towns and Colleges

Britain contains many reminders of the Middle Ages, most particularly in the ancient university cities of Oxford and Cambridge and at places such as Winchester, St Andrews, York and Chester. These widespread locations contain fine examples of Romanesque and Gothic architecture, together with the exquisite craftsmanship that is the hallmark of medieval Britain, be it in wood, stone or glass, painting, weaving or sculpture.

Despite limitations of transport, people travelled widely in the Middle Ages, on pilgrimages, the Crusades, or on official government business. They brought back to Britain the culture of the whole civilised world, inspiring a rich vein of creativity financed by royalty, the nobility, the church, and a growing number of prosperous merchants anxious to display their wealth and generosity. Fortunately much of this artistry still exists today.

Christ Church, Oxford (right), was founded by Cardinal Wolsey before his fall from grace as Henry VIII's chancellor. Above the entrance gate looms Tom Tower. Every evening at 9.05 its bell, Great Tom, tolls 101 times, the number of students in the original foundation plus a studentship added in 1663.

Villages in the Cotswolds prospered during the Middle Ages through the wool trade, their mills powered by fast-flowing streams. Following the invention of the steam-driven loom, the textile trade moved to northern England, leaving places like Castle Combe (below) in a medieval time-warp.

The Cross in Chester, with its half-timbered houses, lies at the heart of this glorious medieval city. Chester's name derives from the Roman Castra Devena, 'the camp on the Dee', the river on which it lies. Chester is the only English city to retain its entire ancient city wall.

An aerial view of Oxford shows how well the university area of the city, with its famous 'dreaming spires', has maintained its medieval appearance. Oxford is Britain's oldest university: its scholars were teaching here in the 12th century. Its students have ranged from Oscar Wilde to Margaret Thatcher.

Medieval Towns and Colleges

The chapel at King's College, Cambridge, was completed by Henry VIII after construction had been considerably delayed by the long-running Wars of the Roses. On the left of the chapel lies Clare, Cambridge's second oldest college, financed by Lady Elizabeth de Clare in 1338.

The poet Lord Byron kept a bear in his rooms at Trinity College, Cambridge, claiming it was more intelligent than his tutors.

Winchester has a long history: Alfred the Great was crowned king of Wessex here in 871; in medieval times, the Great Hall (above) was built during the reign of Henry III; in the mid 14th century the Black Death wiped out more than half the town's population; and Winchester College, one of Britain's top schools, was founded in 1387.

King Henry VIII formed Trinity College, Cambridge, by combining two far older colleges, Michaelhouse and King's Hall, the latter founded by Edward III in 1336. Edward's statue and coat of arms remains on the original gateway into his college, the first of Cambridge's many gatehouses.

Medieval Towns and Colleges

The Shambles in York is one of the best preserved medieval streets in Europe. For 900 years it was a street of butchers but today is crammed with gift shops for the three million tourists who visit this superb northern medieval city each year.

MOORS, MOUNTAINS AND COUNTRYSIDE

Britain possesses a remarkably varied landscape, from the rugged uplands of northern and western regions to the flat wetlands of the Somerset Levels and Norfolk Broads. Snow can remain on Ben Nevis, Britain's highest mountain at 1,343 metres (4,406 feet), for much of the year, whilst vineyards flourish in the Weald of Kent.

Considering the density of Britain's population, surprisingly large areas of unspoilt moors, mountains and beautiful countryside still exist. Much of this landscape has been unchanged for centuries, and provides a haven for wildlife, from the untamed ponies of Dartmoor and the New Forest to the Scottish eagle and capercaillie, the latter being the largest game bird in Europe. The unique character of such areas has been preserved through the creation of National Parks and Areas of Outstanding Natural Beauty.

Glencoe in the Scottish Highlands was the scene of the infamous massacre of members of the MacDonald clan by the treacherous Campbells in 1692. The area still retains a chilling air of menace, particularly on dark and stormy days.

The delightful combination of lochs and rugged mountains is one of the unique features of the Scottish Highlands. To the north of Perth, the view across Loch Tay to Ben Lawers, the highest peak in the Grampians, presents Scotland at its best.

In late spring the lake is often still completely frozen and the sheer sides of Cader Idris in west Wales are covered in ice, providing challenging conditions for the many mountaineers who climb here. Cader Idris means 'Idris's chair', Idris being either a legendary giant or an ancient Welsh chieftain.

Rushup Edge is in the Peak District in Derbyshire, close to the Pennine Way. This popular, long-distance walk stretches 400 kilometres (250 miles), from Edale, near Derby, to the Scottish Borders.

Moors, Mountains and Countryside

Dartmoor is a huge area of majestic upland covered with rocky outcrops, known as tors. Here Dartmoor ponies still roam wild and picturesque villages, such as Buckland in the Moor (left), huddle in deep valleys, called combes.

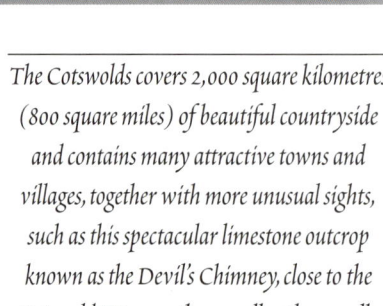

The Cotswolds covers 2,000 square kilometres (800 square miles) of beautiful countryside and contains many attractive towns and villages, together with more unusual sights, such as this spectacular limestone outcrop known as the Devil's Chimney, close to the Cotswold Way, another excellent long walk.

The giant eagle owl has been seen swooping over northern England and Scotland once more.

Moors, Mountains and Countryside

This windpump at Thurne is one of many in the Norfolk Broads, a magnificent expanse of small lakes linked by narrow rivers wriggling through tall reeds – perfect conditions for messing about in boats.

The rugged beauty of the Lake District in the north-west of England is ensured by its designation as a National Park. The road from Windermere over Kirkstone Pass, past Brother's Water, Ullswater and the mountain of Helvellyn to Keswick on Derwent Water is a particularly attractive route.

Its wingspan is up to 1.5 metres (5 feet) across.

Moors, Mountains and Countryside

The Weald of Kent has long been an area for brewing beer from locally grown hops, which were once roasted in these typical oast houses. Those shown here are near Lamberhurst which also boasts England's largest vineyard.

Wiltshire, one of England's lesser known counties, is largely unspoilt. Its distinctive white horses were carved in the chalk uplands to mark historic events. The horse at Westbury, for example, was originally created to celebrate a victory by King Arthur over the Danes in the 9th century.

ROYAL RESIDENCES

Unlike many other countries in Europe Britain remains a monarchy, with royal residences that are homes for the Queen and the Royal Family and not just museums. The monarch retains palaces in both London and Edinburgh that are also used for official business. The age of royal residences varies greatly from Windsor, which was founded by William the Conqueror, and Hampton Court, built in Tudor times, to Sandringham in Norfolk, which is little more than 100 years old.

England's greatest architects have been involved in their construction or extension: Inigo Jones designed the Queen's House in Greenwich, John Nash enlarged Buckingham Palace, while Christopher Wren developed Kensington Palace and Hampton Court. They are treasure houses of great paintings, tapestries and furniture. Many royal residences are open to the public for large parts of the year, giving the public access to an important part of our national heritage.

In 1821 George IV commissioned his favourite architect, John Nash, to enlarge Buckingham Palace. Today it is the main residence of the sovereign and used by the Queen as both home and office. Although extensively used for state occasions and official entertaining, the palace is open to the public during the summer.

Windsor Castle has been an official royal palace since Norman times. Although it is often used by the Queen, a major part of the castle including the State Apartments and St George's Chapel are regularly open to the public.

ROYAL RESIDENCES

Hampton Court was first used as a royal residence by Henry VIII. It was considerably extended during the reign of William III to designs drawn up by Christopher Wren. Subsequent monarchs preferred Buckingham Palace or Windsor as their London residence, enabling Hampton Court, its maze and gardens to become a major tourist attraction.

Kensington Palace was developed by Christopher Wren as a royal palace during the late 17th century. It is still used by several members of the Royal Family, including Diana, Princess of Wales, until her death. Kensington Palace also houses a major exhibition of Court and ceremonial dress through the ages.

ROYAL RESIDENCES

In 1542 Catherine Howard, Henry VIII's fifth wife, was taken from Hampton Court to the Tower of London for execution. It is said that her ghost has been heard shrieking in Hampton Court's Haunted Gallery.

Holyroodhouse Palace in Edinburgh is the sovereign's official royal residence in Scotland. Over the centuries Holyroodhouse has been progressively transformed from a medieval fortress into an elegant baroque residence.

Sandringham in Norfolk has been a favourite home of the Royal Family since it was bought by the Prince of Wales before he became Edward VII. The Queen's father, George VI, wrote, 'I have always been happy here and I love the place.' Royal Christmases are usually held at Sandringham.

Stately Homes and Gardens

Britain contains an impressive number of stately homes covering virtually every period of the nation's architectural history. Whilst many of these are now owned by The National Trust, others still remain in private hands, often owned and lived in by the very same families who originally commissioned great architects, such as Smythson, Vanbrugh, Kent and Adam, to build them. They are filled with the works of the world's greatest artists and craftsmen: Gainsborough, Canaletto, Van Dyke, Grinling Gibbons, Sheraton and Chippendale.

A grateful monarch, Queen Anne, granted the Duke of Marlborough both land and a large sum of money in recognition of his victory over the French and Bavarian armies at Blenheim near Vienna in 1704. John Vanbrugh created this magnificent house near Oxford surrounded by a park designed by Capability Brown.

Equally impressive are the huge variety of gardens ranging from Capability Brown's Arcadian landscaped parks to the floral splendour of Wisley and the formally designed gardens of Gertrude Jekyll and Edwin Lutyens. Originally these stately homes and gardens were the private indulgences of a few wealthy and privileged aristocrats, but today they are available to everyone to marvel at their glory.

'I would not exceed the limits of expense that I have set myself. Let us do everything properly and well, mais pas trop,*' Edwin Lascalles, the 18th-century owner of Harewood, commanded Robert Adam. The result was this superb Yorkshire house.

Hatfield House in Hertfordshire was given by James I to Sir Robert Cecil in exchange for the latter's nearby home of Theobolds. Cecil replaced the old Tudor building with an imposing Jacobean residence. The gardens have been extensively restored by the present Marchioness of Salisbury.

Bess of Hardwick built Chatsworth in 1552, and it has been lived in by the Cavendish family, the Dukes of Devonshire, ever since. It displays work by Verrio, William Kent, Rembrandt, Van Dyke, Tintoretto and others – this *trompe l'oeil* violin can be seen in the music room. The garden has a spectacular water cascade and fountain.

Stately Homes and Gardens

Henry VIII acquired additional homes simply by confiscating them from their owners – Thornbury Castle, Penshurst Place and Knole are just three examples.

Castle Howard in Yorkshire (right) was built by John Vanbrugh for the Earl of Carlisle in 1699. Although it was Vanbrugh's first attempt at designing a house, he succeeded in creating a masterpiece. The dramatic Atlas Fountain was installed in the mid 19th century.

Situated on the shores of the Firth of Forth near Edinburgh, the 18th-century Hopetoun House (above) is considered to be Scotland's finest stately home. Set in 40 hectares (100 acres) of parkland, Hopetoun is the home of the Marquess of Linlithgow.

STATELY HOMES AND GARDENS

The headquarters of the Royal Horticultural Society have been located at Wisley in Surrey since 1904. The 100-hectare (240-acre) garden is a magnificent showpiece for the Society and includes an arboretum, glasshouses and Mediterranean garden. Wisley is open throughout the year.

The 121 hectares (300 acres) of Kew Gardens in Surrey include a number of grand glasshouses: the Palm House is 20 metres (65 feet) high, while the Temperate and Tropical Houses are equally impressive. Kew is also famous for its Chinese Pagoda built by Sir William Chambers in the reign of George III.

Exbury, on the shores of the River Beaulieu in Hampshire, is renowned for its rhododendrons and azaleas. It was created in the 1920s and 30s by Lionel Nathan de Rothschild, a member of the famous banking family. According to his son Edmund, de Rothschild was 'a banker by hobby and gardener by profession'.

Stately Homes and Gardens

Henry Hoare, a banker and enthusiastic amateur gardener, created Stourhead, an exceptional garden arranged around a huge lake, in the mid 18th century. It contains a series of classical buildings such as the Pantheon and the Temple of Diana. Open throughout the year, each season has a distinctive appeal.

Henry Hoare created Stourhead out of the profits of his 18th-century London bank. Stourhead's present-day Henry Hoare is chairman of Britain's last privately owned family bank.

The present owner of Longleat is the 7th Marquess of Bath. More than 400 years ago his ancestor Sir John Thynne, a former kitchen clerk in the Tudor royal palace, created this great example of the English Renaissance. The exterior remains virtually unaltered since that time.

Stately Homes and Gardens

Considered to be England's finest arboretum, Westonbirt is in the Cotswolds in Gloucestershire. Originally conceived by Captain Robert Holford in 1829, Westonbirt is now owned by the Forestry Commission. It looks superb in autumn when the acers are at their vibrant best.

Scone Palace was built on the foundations of Scone Abbey, destroyed in the Reformation. It was here that Scottish kings including Macbeth and Robert the Bruce were crowned. The magnificent grounds, which stretch down to the River Tay, contain the original Douglas fir, Highland cattle and peacocks.

Rivers, Canals and Lakes

Britain's rainfall ensures a large variety of rivers and estuaries, from rushing mountain torrents and trickling trout streams to large, winding rivers such as Old Father Thames.

Before the construction of railways and tarred roads, rivers and canals provided a vital way to transport commercial goods across the country. Today both rivers and canals are well used for leisure pursuits, such as catching salmon, or enjoying a holiday aboard a narrowboat as it chugs down a canal through unspoilt countryside. Lakes are a tranquil addition to the landscape and provide a marvellous habitat for a wide range of wildlife.

Crossing these waterways are a huge variety of bridges – ingenious feats of engineering and soaring sculptural shapes that are as much works of art as functional objects.

The Wye is one of Britain's most beautiful rivers, flowing through attractive countryside on the Welsh border, and towns such as Ross on Wye, Monmouth and Chepstow. The river provides excellent salmon fishing and fine walks on Offa's Dyke and in the Wye Valley.

The Forth Rail Bridge was built in 1890, near Edinburgh, to take trains across the Firth of Forth. Bridges in this part of Britain must be extremely strong: in 1879 a gale destroyed the bridge over the nearby River Tay, plunging a train and its passengers into the river below.

Tower Bridge was built in the late 19th century when the City of London was a thriving port and large vessels berthed in the adjoining St Katharine's Dock. Today this major landmark houses 'The Tower Bridge Experience' – a history of the area – and the drawbridges are still raised to allow tall ships to sail through.

Rivers, Canals and Lakes

In the late 1600s, temperatures in Britain dropped so low the River Thames in London froze for several winters running.

Travelling by water can be leisurely and relaxing. Traditional narrowboats provide a slow but fascinating journey along Britain's canals (above), but punting a flat-bottomed boat with one long pole (left) is deceptively difficult!

Queen Victoria was once rowed the entire length (22 kilometres, or 14 miles) of Loch Tay in the Highlands of Perthshire. The small town of Kenmore lies where the loch narrows into the River Tay. Here, Robert Burns, Scotland's foremost poet, has written a poem on the wall of the inn.

The Calstock Viaduct in Cornwall, like Isambard Brunel's Tamar Bridge further downstream, was built to take the railway across the river which divides Devon and Cornwall – or England and Cornwall, as the Cornish prefer to say.

Rivers, Canals and Lakes

The 19th-century Clifton Suspension Bridge over the Avon Gorge at Bristol was one of Isambard Brunel's many spectacular engineering feats. He also designed Paddington Station and the giant ship SS Great Britain, which can be seen in Bristol.

Historic Towns and Cities

After the Middle Ages the nation's population grew quickly, and manufacturing and commerce overtook agriculture as the main source of employment. The middle classes expanded rapidly, and better education produced a more sophisticated society with more time for leisure. As a result, many of Britain's towns greatly enlarged, and in the 18th century a new phenomena called tourism began.

Nowhere was this more evident than in the Georgian spa towns of Bath, Cheltenham, Harrogate and Tunbridge Wells, where society gathered to take the waters, to 'see and be seen'. This led to the construction of elegant town houses, imposing civic buildings designed by the leading architects of the day, spacious squares and sweeping crescents, many of which remain today. Elsewhere Shakespeare had already popularised Stratford-on-Avon, Edinburgh became Scotland's most fashionable city, and Brighton developed as an early seaside resort.

Plymouth is an historic port. This statue of Sir Francis Drake, the naval hero of England's victory over the Spanish Armada in 1588, stands on Plymouth Hoe. Plymouth is now the largest naval base in western Europe, but the Barbican and Sutton Harbour, where Drake, Raleigh and Hawkins anchored their ships in Tudor times, remains.

Over the centuries Bristol has been a port trading in slaves and a centre for the tobacco and wine industries as well as aircraft manufacturing – Concorde first flew from nearby Filton. These elegant period houses can still be seen in the historic area of Clifton.

Shakespeare made the ancient town of Stratford-on-Avon a one-man tourist attraction: it contains his birthplace (above) and many other attractive half-timbered buildings associated with him. The world-famous Royal Shakespeare Theatre, where his work is frequently performed by Britain's finest actors, is on the bank of the River Avon.

Bath became fashionable during the 18th century. High Society flocked here to take the waters, gamble and party. John Wood the Younger began the Royal Crescent in 1767, whilst Pitt, Livingstone, Gainsborough and Clive of India all lived in the Circus, built by Wood the Elder.

Historic Towns and Cities

The Prince Regent originally went to Brighton because his father King George III would not allow him to travel more than 80 kilometres (50 miles) from London.

Originally known as 'Brighthelmstone', this one-time fishing village was re-named Brighton when the Prince Regent, later George IV, made it fashionable with his frequent visits. The Brighton Pavilion, inspired by the orient, was designed by John Nash in 1782.

Historic Towns and Cities

Choristers Green in Salisbury. Salisbury was created as a medieval 'new town', and built on a gridiron pattern around the cathedral whose foundation stone was laid in 1220. Both town and cathedral suffered during the Civil War, but revived after the Restoration, as shown by extensive building during the late 17th and early 18th centuries.

Edinburgh, the capital of Scotland, is a major cultural centre, famous for its annual Festival. The Festival includes the colourful Edinburgh Tattoo, held in the ancient fortress of Castle Rock, the site of the original settlement in Roman times.

The city of Lincoln rises like an island from the exceedingly flat countryside of eastern England. A long street full of historic buildings winds uphill to England's earliest Gothic cathedral. This fine statue of Tennyson, the Lincolnshire born poet, with his dog is in the Close.

Among Scotland's many eminent men is Charles Rennie Mackintosh, the art nouveau architect who designed the celebrated Argyll Street tea rooms and ground-breaking School of Art in Glasgow.

Traditions and Ceremonies

Nothing delights and bemuses visitors to Britain more than the enormously varied and colourful traditions and ceremonies which form an intrinsic part of Britain's heritage. Some are regular events, such as Changing the Guard at Buckingham Palace and at Windsor, others take place annually and include the Eisteddfod, the Edinburgh Tattoo, the Oxford and Cambridge Boat Race, the London to Brighton Car Run, and the Glastonbury Festival.

Some rituals date back to pagan times; others are more recent and, like the Notting Hill Carnival, reflect Britain's growing multi-cultural society. Many ancient customs appear completely bizarre to the outsider, yet most are unique to Britain, and are popular with participants and with visitors alike.

Trooping the Colour at Horse Guard's Parade in London celebrates the Queen's official birthday in early June. This spectacular annual event includes a display of marching by the regiments of the Brigade of Guards to the music of massed bands. Although usually seen in ceremonial dress, these regiments, including the Coldstreams which first formed in the Civil War, remain crack fighting troops in the 21st century.

A highly colourful and ancient custom is the parade of the judiciary at the start of the Legal Year. On 1 October, dressed in traditional wigs and robes, they attend a special service at Westminster Abbey and then walk in procession to the Houses of Parliament for the Lord Chancellor's Breakfast.

A large number of veteran cars set off from Hyde Park in London to drive to Brighton on the first Sunday in November. The tradition began in 1896 to celebrate the abolition of the law which required vehicles to drive at less than 4 miles per hour proceeded by a man on foot.

An opportunity to see the Queen always draws a crowd, particularly when she rides in a ceremonial carriage accompanied by horsemen of the Household Cavalry to events such as the State Opening of Parliament or, as here, from the Garter service in St George's Chapel in Windsor Castle.

Traditions and Ceremonies

A recent but fast growing and popular event is the Bristol Balloon Festival. Held in August each year, it is the largest of its kind in Britain, with hundreds of balloons of all shapes and sizes taking part. The massed launch is an unforgettable sight.

It is customary to stand to drink the Loyal Toast to the monarch, except in the Royal Navy where officers have been allowed to remain seated since the days of low headroom in sailing ships.

Traditions and Ceremonies

A group of Civil War enthusiasts known as the Sealed Knot Society recreate 17th-century battles between the Royalists and Parliamentarian armies, very often on the sites of the original battles. These colourful and exciting events are highly authentic and historically accurate in every detail.

Popular both with locals and visitors, the inn, public house, or simply 'pub', is one of Britain's favourite and time-honoured institutions. Many are gems of vernacular architecture, often with highly unusual names. Today most provide excellent food and many provide rooms where all the family can enjoy a meal together.

Each February the citizens of York celebrate the conquest of York by the Vikings in 866. The Vikings called the city 'Jorvik' and the Jorvik Viking Festival includes torchlit parades (below) and a longship regatta held on the River Ouse.

Traditions and Ceremonies

Eisteddfods are a traditional Welsh gathering of music, poetry and literature. The National Eisteddfod takes place annually and lasts seven to ten days, ending with an award ceremony, one category being the best contestant in verse, known as 'chairing the bard'.

On the last weekend of every August, London's Caribbean community runs a carnival in the area of Notting Hill which rivals that of Rio de Janeiro for its joyful dancing, music and extravagant costumes. More than a million people enjoy the spectacle, said to be the largest street party in Europe.

Traditions and Ceremonies

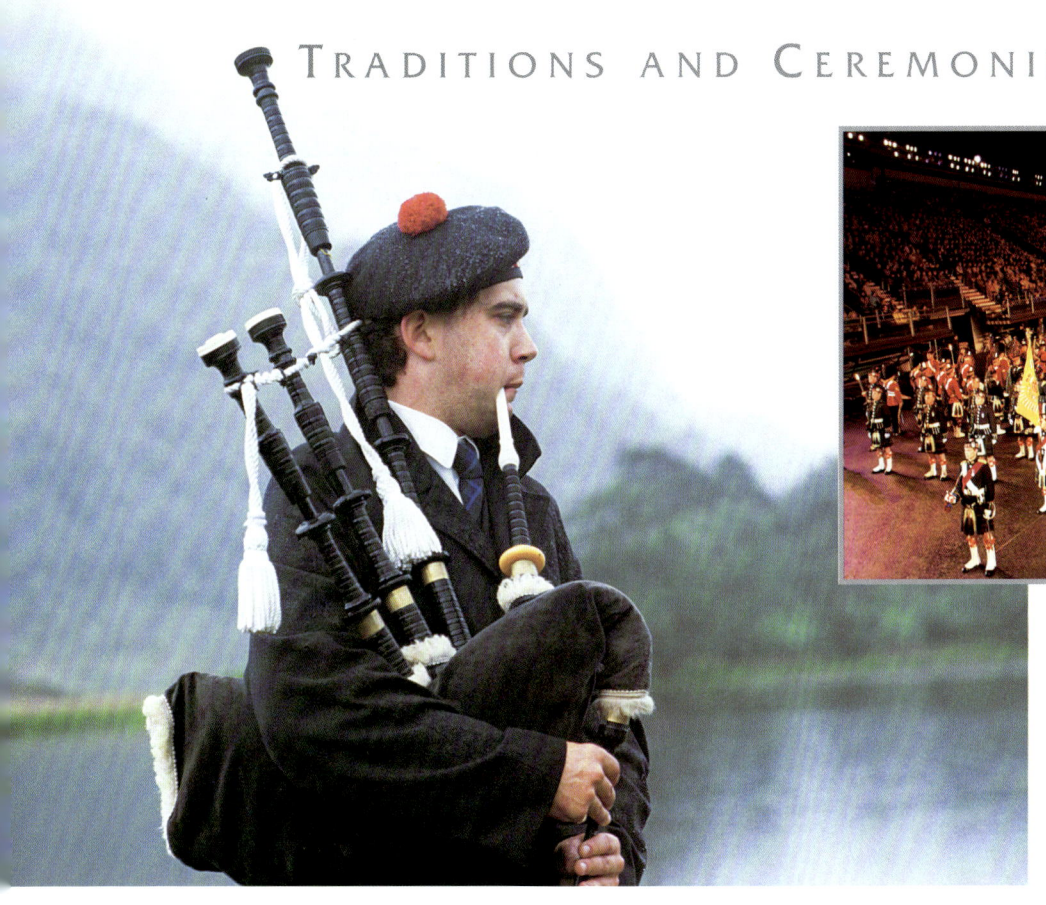

The skirl of the bagpipes is a stirring sound, whether they are played by a solitary Scottish piper at the Highland Games or in a massed band at events such as the Edinburgh Tattoo (above).

'Fair, fa' your honest, sonsie face,/ Great chieftain o' the puddin-race!'
The opening lines of the address to the haggis, recited at Burns Night Suppers on 25 January to honour Scotland's greatest poet. Haggis is a traditional Scottish dish of oatmeal and offal.

Fans from all over Britain flock to Glastonbury each year to listen to rock music and soak up the atmosphere. Each June they camp out for several days whatever the weather – seasoned festival-goers never fail to come well prepared for rain!

Coasts and Seaside

Britain consists of a large island surrounded by numerous smaller ones, which range from the semi-tropical Isles of Scilly, to rugged windswept reefs pounded by surf. Some are thriving communities, others uninhabited, yet all provide ideal habitat for a variety of birdlife – sea eagles, cormorants, gannets and puffins. An increasing amount of Britain's coastline is now owned by The National Trust, ensuring that its soaring cliffs and sandy coves will be preserved, a coast where sailors and surfers have replaced the smugglers and wreckers of the past.

Nowhere in Britain is far from the sea. With the coming of the railways in the 19th century, people of all classes were able to leave the smoke-filled cities and escape to the coast for a bank holiday or a week at the sea. Holiday resorts, with entertainment on the pier and donkey rides on the beach, boomed. Even today, when foreign holidays are so popular, many Britons still enjoy a traditional family holiday at the seaside.

This amazing rock formation in the Orkneys off the northernmost tip of the Scottish mainland is known as the Old Man of Hoy – from the Norse for 'High Island'. This 140-metre (450-foot) high rock stack provides a formidable challenge to even the most skilled rock-climbers.

The Sussex Downs rise up above the English Channel, creating the white cliffs of Dover and some dramatic coastal scenery. These chalk cliffs, known as the Seven Sisters, are to the east of Brighton near Beachy Head.

The Isles of Scilly, off Lands End in Cornwall, are England's most westerly inhabited islands: beyond them lies the vast Atlantic Ocean. The islands have incredibly white sand and turquoise water.

St Ives in west Cornwall is popular with artists who are attracted to the scenery and unique quality of light. The little fishing harbour is centuries old and delights those who come to visit. Nearby is Lands End, the most westerly point in England.

Coasts and Seaside

Lighthouses are a common sight around the British Isles. They warn of nautical dangers, such as this treacherous but beautiful outcrop known as The Needles, off the Isle of Wight.

This eye-catching striped lighthouse at Portland Bill is well known to sailors navigating the English Channel. Below the headland flows the Portland race, a hazardous tidal current.

The pier at Llandudno in Gwynedd, north Wales, is one of many similar structures which became popular at seaside resorts around Britain in the 19th century.

Coasts and Seaside

Weymouth on the Dorset coast became a popular tourist resort in the 19th century when King George III bathed here. Today, the traditional delights of Punch and Judy, donkey rides and candyfloss continue to pull in the crowds.

Britain's most popular beaches can become exceedingly crowded, but others, like this stretch of silver sand near Cromer (left) on the north Norfolk coast, remain empty even during the height of the season.

Punch and Judy shows have been performed in Britain for many centuries. Pepys recorded in his diary seeing a performance in May 1662. A plaque in Covent Garden records the event.

Blakeney in north Norfolk is one of numerous towns and villages in eastern England identified by a distinctive sign. A sailor with a distinctive eyepatch from this part of the world was Horatio Nelson, born at nearby Burnham Thorpe in 1758. He went to sea at the tender age of 12.

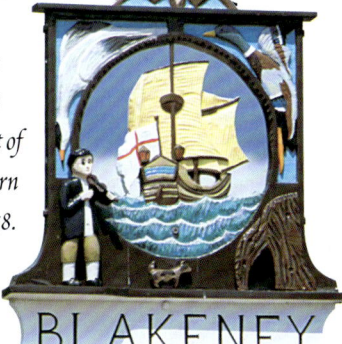

Modern Britain

Britain may well be an ancient kingdom, steeped in history and proud of its heritage, but it is by no means a prisoner of the past. The old transforms into the new: at the beginning of the 21st century Britain is a dynamic, modern country at the cutting edge of art and technology, design, cinema, computerisation and medical science. Its actors, architects, inventors, sportsmen and women, fashion models and rock musicians are famous throughout the world.

Many new landmarks catch the eye, in London and across the nation. Britain is a constantly changing, lively place, full of wit and understanding, confident yet unconventional – an exciting place to be in the new Millennium.

The second Severn Bridge crosses the Bristol Channel to link England and Wales. This architectural masterpiece is also an incredible feat of engineering, designed to withstand the huge tidal rise and fall and strong currents of the River Severn.

Motorists travelling up the A1 towards Newcastle are surprised when first glimpsing Antony Gormley's giant sculpture, the Angel of the North. Sculpture has often been used to enhance the landscape and Gormley follows Henry Moore, Barbara Hepworth and Anthony Caro in a long line of modern British sculptors.

The new Eurostar Station at Waterloo is the terminus for passengers using the fast rail link through the Channel Tunnel to Europe. Nicholas Grimshaw's building is the modern equivalent of Victorian railway termini such as Isambard Brunel's Paddington Station – a soaring hall of metal and glass.

The giant, slowly revolving wheel known as British Airways London Eye was erected on the South Bank of the River Thames to mark the Millennium. The view from the cars provides a panoramic vision of the nation's capital city, a unique view of such famous sights as the River Thames, the Houses of Parliament and St Paul's Cathedral.

Modern Britain

Dynamic Earth in Edinburgh takes visitors through 4,500 million years of the Earth's history using devices such as a time machine and a yellow submarine. It was designed by Sir Michael Hopkins and opened in 1999 with Edinburgh's own extinct volcano, Arthur's Seat, providing a dramatic backdrop.

Tim Smit, who restored the Lost Gardens of Heligan in Cornwall, subsequently commissioned Nicholas Grimshaw to create the Eden Project, a giant pair of linked 'covered biomes', greenhouses containing temperate and tropical plants, on the site of a former Cornish china clay pit near St Austell.

Modern Britain

The new Media Centre, built to accommodate television commentators and the press at Lord's Cricket Ground in St John's Wood, London, was awarded the prestigious Stirling Prize by the Royal Institute of British Architects in 1999. It is interesting that the usually ultra-conservative MCC should commission such an avant-garde building.

The Eden Project's humid tropics biome covers 15,590 square metres (18,646 square yards) – more than the area of two football pitches – making it the largest greenhouse in the world.

Tate Modern in London stands on the south bank of the Thames. The building, once the gigantic Bankside Power Station, has been brilliantly converted into an exciting space to display the nation's collection of modern art from 1900 to the present day, including this huge spider by Louise Bourgeoise.

The slender and graceful 325-metre (1066ft) steel Millennium Bridge, the first pedestrian bridge to be built across the Thames in the centre of London for over 100 years, spans the river from St Paul's Cathedral in the City of London to the Tate Modern at Bankside.

INDEX

Bath 4, 12, 13, 46, 47, BC
Battle Abbey 6
Big Ben 1, 9
Blenheim, Battle of 9
Bleinheim Palace 10, 36
Bodiam Castle 16
Brighton 46, 48, 50, 51, 57
Bristol 45, 46, 52
British Airways London Eye 61
Buckingham Palace 33, 34, 50

Cader Idris 29
Caernarfon Castle 6–7
Caerphilly Castle 15
Callinish 12
Cambridge 8, 24, 26
Canterbury Cathedral 18
Castle Howard 10, 38
Chatsworth House 37
Chester 21, 24, 25
Civil War 9, 17, 49, 50, 53
Clifton Suspension Bridge 45
Conwy Castle 15
Cornwall 44, 57, 62, 63
Cotswolds 24, 30, 41
Cromer 59
Cromwell, Oliver 9, 14

Dark Ages 6, 12
Dartmoor 12, 17, 28, 30
Dover Castle 14
Drake, Sir Francis 8, 46
Dunvegan Castle 15
Durham Cathedral 7, 22

Edinburgh 35, 46, 49, 50, 55, 62
Eisteddfod 50, 54
Elizabeth I 8
Elizabeth II 19, 33, 35, 50, 51
Exbury 39

Forth Rail Bridge 43

Glasgow 49
Globe Theatre 8
Gloucester Cathedral 23

Hadrian's Wall 12, 13
Hampton Court 33, 34, 35
Harewood House 37
Harlech Castle 17
Hatfield House 37
Henry VIII 8, 20, 24, 26, 34, 38
HMS *Victory* 10
Hopetoun House 10, 38
Houghton Hall 10
Houses of Parliament 9, 50

Iona 13
Isles of Scilly 56, 57

Kensington Palace 33, 34

Lake District 31
Lincoln 18, 49
Llandudno 58
Longleat 8, 40
Lord's Cricket Ground 63

Medieval Britain 6–7, 14, 18, 24
Melrose Abbey 22
Millennium Bridge 63

Nelson's Column 4, 5
Norfolk 33, 35, 59
Norfolk Broads 28, 31

Orkneys 56
Oxford 8, 24, 25

Peak District 29
Pentre Ifan 12

Railways 10, 61
Rievaulx Abbey 18

Robert the Bruce 7, 22, 41
Romans 12, 13, 25, 49

St Davids Cathedral 21
St Paul's Cathedral 10, 22
Salisbury 20, 49
Sandringham 33, 35
Scone Palace 41
Scottish Highlands 10, 28, 29, 44
Second World War 11, 14
Severn Bridge 60
Shakespeare, William 8, 46, 47
Skye, Isle of 2–3, 4, 15
Stonehenge FC, 4, 12
Stourhead 40
Stratford-on-Avon 46, 47
Sudeley Castle 17

Tate Modern 63
Thames, River 22, 42, 44, 61
Tintern Abbey 20
Tower Bridge 43
Tower of London 7, 14
Trafalgar, Battle of 4, 10
Tudors 8, 33, 46

Wars of the Roses 7, 17
Warwick Castle 17
Weald of Kent 28, 32
Wells Cathedral 21
Westminster Abbey 6, 19
Westonbirt 41
White horse, Westbury 32
William the Conqueror 6, 7, 14, 17, 19, 33
Winchester 22, 24, 26
Windsor Castle 33, 50, 51
Wisley 36, 39
Wren, Christopher 10, 22, 33, 34
Wye, River 42

York 10, 17, 18, 24, 27, 53